The Song of Love

MANISH WADHWA

Disclaimer:
This book descended from my Heart.
If any of my words or works of art,
have any resemblance in any part,
to any pre-existing words or art,
consider it to be pure coincidence,
and this I say with full confidence.
I intend only Love, and no feelings hurt,
hence this short poem of disclaimer alert.
This book is Love's abode.
Leaving behind ego's load,
enter the shrine with a pure loving Heart.
This book is not mere words and art….

Copyright © 2020 Manish Wadhwa.
All rights reserved. No part of this publication may be reproduced, distributed, or transmitted in any form or by any means, including photocopying, recording, or other electronic or mechanical methods, without the prior written permission, except in the case of brief quotations embodied in articles and reviews.

ISBN 13: 978-1-7354027-1-0 (B&W Paperback)
Also available in these formats:
ISBN 13: 978-1-7354027-2-7 (Full Color Paperback)
ISBN 13: 978-1-7354027-0-3 (eBook)
ISBN 13: 978-1-7354027-3-4 (B&W Hardcover)

Library of Congress Control Number: 2020915976

Wise Heart Tree Publishing, Peabody, MA, USA.
wisehearttree.com

Illustrations and Design by Manish Wadhwa.
manishwadhwa.com

....Dedicated to Love....

Rosary Beads

	Introduction: The Rosary of Love	*ix*
1.	*The Song of Love*	*1*
2.	*I Am a Flute of Love*	*3*
3.	*Love is – Not of this Dimension*	*5*
4.	*The Embrace of Love*	*7*
5.	*The Fire of Love*	*8*
6.	*Immortal Love*	*10*
7.	*Love: The Magnum Opus*	*11*
8.	*Love: The Eternal Law*	*13*
9.	*Tale of Love*	*14*
10.	*Love I Carry*	*16*
11.	*Love's Glance*	*17*
12.	*Glories of Love*	*19*
13.	*We are Old Lovers*	*20*
14.	*The Image of Love*	*22*
15.	*One Love*	*23*
16.	*Be the Love*	*25*
17.	*Love is Fragrance*	*26*
18.	*Love's Embrace*	*28*
19.	*Love Evaporates*	*29*
20.	*Love is: One Heart Perfected*	*31*
21.	*Love is Loud*	*32*
22.	*Hunt of Love*	*33*
23.	*Love is all I deal with*	*34*
24.	*Jewel of Love*	*36*
25.	*The Freedom of Love*	*38*
26.	*Love: The Heart's only Desire*	*39*
27.	*Love is Worship*	*40*

28.	*Harbinger of Love*	*42*
29.	*Love Is*	*43*
30.	*In Love you are Born*	*45*
31.	*Ambers of Love*	*46*
32.	*The Gaze of Love*	*47*
33.	*The Wine of Love*	*49*
34.	*Love is my Earning*	*51*
35.	*The Peace of Love*	*52*
36.	*Offering of Love*	*54*
37.	*The Fruit of Love*	*55*
38.	*The True Worth of Love*	*57*
39.	*Love Matures*	*58*
40.	*Fragrance of Love*	*60*
41.	*The Essence of Love*	*61*
42.	*The Touch of Love*	*63*
43.	*Love meets Love*	*64*
44.	*The Desert of Love*	*66*
45.	*The God of Love*	*68*
46.	*The Time of Love*	*69*
47.	*The Illusions of Love*	*70*
48.	*The Play of Love*	*71*
49.	*Lover of Love*	*72*
50.	*Waves of Love*	*73*
51.	*Abode of Love*	*75*
52.	*The Whole of Love*	*77*
53.	*Eternity of Love of Eternity*	*79*
54.	*In the Arms of Love*	*80*
55.	*Love's Ode*	*82*
56.	*The Imagination of Love*	*83*
57.	*Nutrition of Love*	*85*
58.	*Hearts of Love*	*86*

59.	Let there be Love	87
60.	Emanations of Love	88
61.	Escapes of Love	91
62.	Love, let's Love	92
63.	The Name of Love	94
64.	The Bird of Love	95
65.	Love is a Kite	96
66.	Love is Waiting	98
67.	What Love Wants	99
68.	Love is Heart's Journey	100
69.	The Abode of Love	101
70.	The Elements of Love	102
71.	The Mirror of Love	104
72.	Love reflects only Love	105
73.	The Nightingale of Love	106
74.	The Incense of Love	108
75.	There is Love	109
76.	Love Blooms	110
77.	Eternal Love	111
78.	Love's Gifts	113
79.	The Doors of Love	114
80.	Love's Demands	116
81.	Love of the Finite	117
82.	The Fabric of Love	118
83.	Love I Enshrine	120
84.	I Became Love	121
85.	May I return to Love	123
86.	This Rose of Love	124
87.	Love Forever	127
88.	Love is Full Circle	128
89.	Love is Nigh	130

90.	Love's Command	131
91.	Love's Rosary	134
92.	Love is the Ultimate Music	135
93.	One God of Love	137
94.	The Tug of Love	138
95.	Reflection of Love	140
96.	Love's Path	141
97.	The Dark Night of Love	142
98.	Love is the Sun	143
99.	Love is all we have	145
100.	To Love and to get Lost	146
101.	Love is the Primal Force	148
102.	Love is in Simple Things	149
103.	In the Honor of Love	151
104.	The Infinity of Love	152
105.	Love is the greatest Phoenix	153
106.	This weird thing called Love	156
107.	I must have Loved	157
108.	The Love's Show	159

Introduction: The Rosary of Love

"The Rosary of Love" presents the very idea behind this book. Writing more would be superfluous.

The Rosary of Love

These Love poems are the beads
of the Rosary of Love divine.
This very poem is the mother bead of Love,
after which begins your inner recitation.

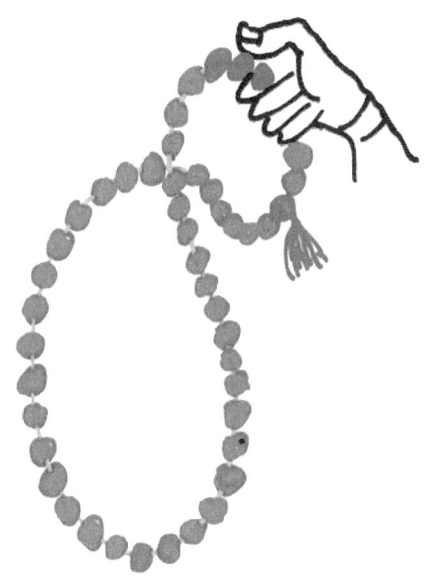

The Infinity of Love is worshipped
through these finite rosary beads.
Read each poem with Hearts open,
ready to receive the bounty of Love.

With every bead of poem,
you pull the thread of Love
running through Heart's every pore.
Our Hearts must be really special!

Mistake it not to the rosary of the hand.
This Rosary of Love is of the Heart.
External symbols are mere suggestions,
the real is worshipped in the Heart.

Each one of us is not
an individual, but the Whole.
Each of these poems is not
an individual, but the Whole.

The rosary of these poems
form the Whole of Love.
This Love within Love
is: The Song of Love.

THE SONG OF LOVE

With every poem you drink,
you fill your Heart's pitcher
with the devotion of Love,
the ever-flowing devotion.

Drink these Love poems
from the cup embellished
with Love and by Love
as: The Song of Love.

MANISH WADHWA

The Song of Love

Come friends,
    gather around.
I will sing a song,
    The Song of Love.

This song is
    heard in silence.
Just relax and
    enjoy the song.

My mouth won't
    utter a single word,
yet my Heart
    will do the trick.

Close your eyes,
    let your Hearts sing along.
In this music,
    our Hearts are a symphony.

This music of the Hearts
   is the music of the Universe.
Listen to the grand opera —
   the magnum opus of Love.

I Am a Flute of Love

I am a flute
on thy lips.
It is thy breath
that gushes through me
and I get awakened.

Again, thy endless strokes
on my reed
sound and resound
a symphony of notes
and I get enlightened.

Thou hast done this
from ages anon.
I am not just —
A piece of reed.
I do not recognize
myself with that.
For I am that that plays me,
and I am that that awakens
and enlightens and frees me.
I know — I AM THAT.

Love is —
Not of this Dimension

My Love is not
of this dimension.

It meets with the Beloved
somewhere beyond.

You want proof,
I do have one.

Someday when you commit
yourself to this journey,

you yourself will be
catapulted to that dimension.

Till then, wonder, research,
and write scholarly articles.

My Love is —
Not of this Dimension.

The Embrace of Love

Love is —
The Eternity's Embrace.

Its arms —
To infinity they extend.

Lover is the Beloved —
Enshrined in the Heart.

From Heart it extends —
To Heart it returns.

This is the mighty —
Embrace of Love.

The Fire of Love

When thousands
of your eyes,
fall upon
my veil,

THE SONG OF LOVE

it waits not
to see another day,
it melts in the
Fire of Love.

Immortal Love

A part in Me
dies every day,
the Whole in Me
lives forever.

When I part from You,
I die a little.
The Whole in Me is You,
the Never Dying.

In the mortality
of my being,
You live but a little.

In the Whole,
You are my
Immortal Love….

Love: The Magnum Opus

Love Is —

The Grandest Design

Love Is —

The Breath Divine

Love Is —

The Summum Bonum

Love Is —

The Cosmic Abdomen

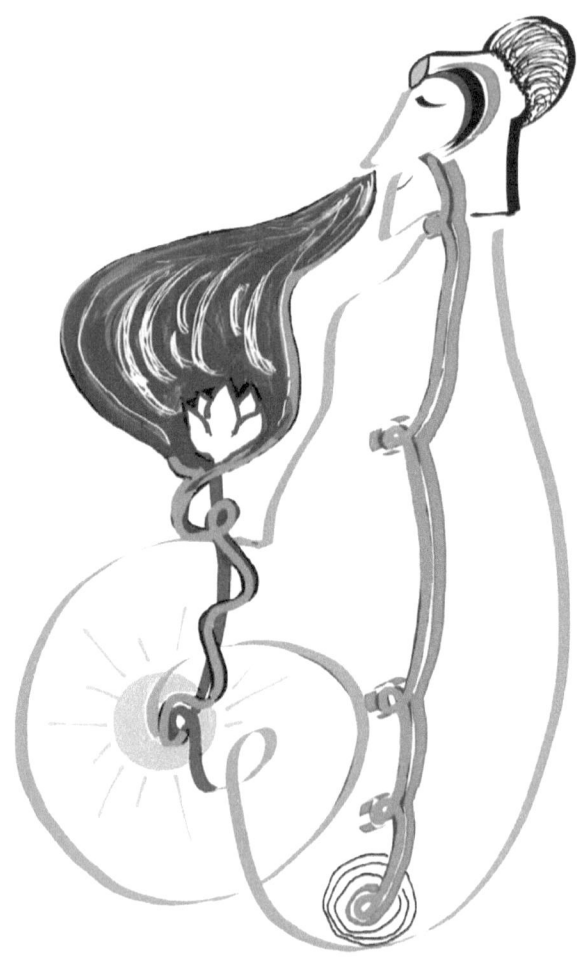

Love Is —

The Divine Lotus

Love Is —

The Magnum Opus

Love: The Eternal Law

For a moment I thought
you abandoned me,
but then I realized
how mistaken I was.

Coming and going
is of the worldly.
This Love is:
The Eternal Law.

Tale of Love

How else could we Love?

If not through
this sweet,
Pain of Love….

If not through
two bodies,
Twain of Love….

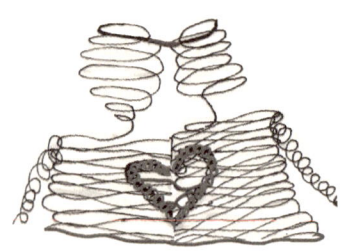

THE SONG OF LOVE

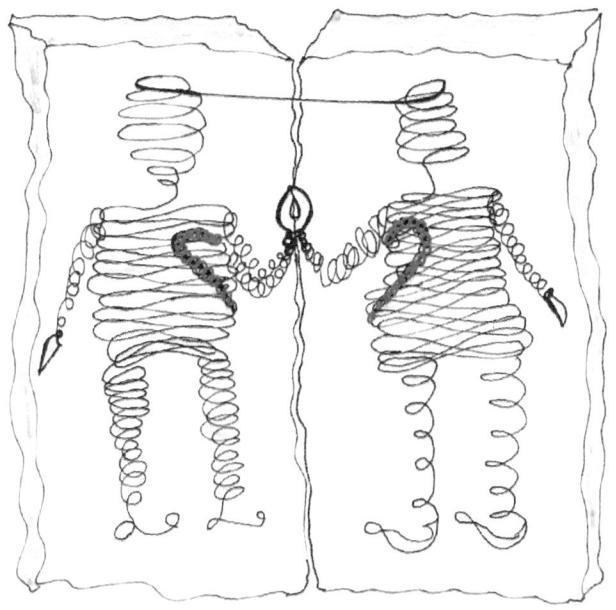

If not through
this separating,
Veil of Love....

If not through
this comforting,
Tale of Love....

Love I Carry

I know not
    thy name,
yet thy name
    alone I know.
In the depths
    of my Heart,
it's thee who
    sing beauty.
I hear thy
    voice beautiful.
It's thee whose
    Love I Carry
in the deepest recesses
    of my Heart.

Love's Glance

My Heart is calling you....
My memories are recalling you....
Love's glance makes you dance.

My yearning is churning me....
My Beloved is burning me....
Love's glance makes you dance.

I love you from ages....
I whirl like Sufi-sages....
Love's glance makes you dance.

In the silence between you and me….
One day I shall become thee….
Love's glance makes you dance.

Our union will be forever….
Then I shall return never….
Love's glance makes you dance.

Glories of Love

All my longings….
All my belongings….
No meaning do they hold,
if I speak not of You
in my Art.

All my yearnings….
All my learnings….
No meaning do they hold,
if I keep You away
from my Heart.

All my cares….
All my prayers….
No meaning do they hold,
if I sing not,
Thy Glories of Love.

We are Old Lovers

Flowers grow in Wilderness
Our Brave Love in Tenderness….

This Love is the Flowering
Of our Eternal Longing….

Since day one of Eternity
We have been in Love….

THE SONG OF LOVE

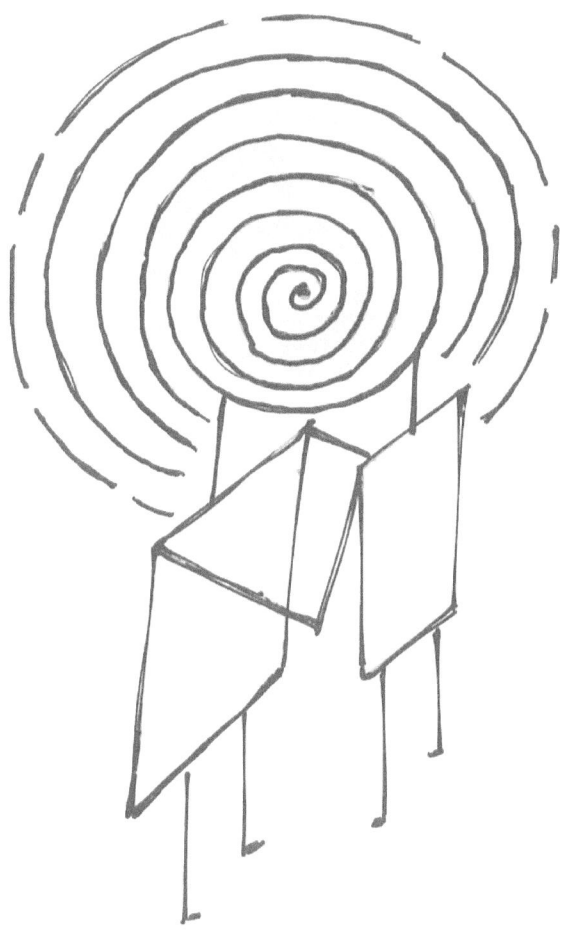

Time shrinks in this Wilderness
We are Old Lovers….

The Image of Love

Love creeps in
from the corners,
where reside
the mirrors of the soul.

These mirrors reflect
the Image of Love.

One Love

I and you are
        a Love affair….

I am you
        and you me….

Still you keep
        the veil intact….

for this Love affair
        to continue forever….

My Heart merges
    with yours….

like waves in water
    they merge….

The separation is false
    we are One….

There is only
    One Love….

Be the Love

Come, my Love,
I will give you something,
something beyond thought.

I may not be with you,
now or ever,
but this Love you Be,
and I will leave you never.

Come, my Love,
I will give you something,
something beyond thought.

Just Be the Love….

Love is Fragrance

Your heart is my heart.
They are One Heart.
There is only One Heart.
Divisions are all illusory.

Love is the beginning,
and so is the end.

Heart is the God —
Love is Godliness.

Heart is the Flower —
Love is Fragrance.

Love's Embrace

My Love for thee
is an ever-widening river,
whose culmination
is an Endless Ocean….

My Love for thee
is an infinite extension.
That is how Lovers Embrace
each other as Eternity….

Love Evaporates

Love's colors
and fragrances
come from tender
Heart-Lotus.

In the hearth
called busyness
of everyday life,
Love Evaporates.

Love is: One Heart Perfected

Our hearts
are interconnected.
As if by a cord
they are connected.
They communicate and
their Love is reflected.
From many a mile
they are affected.
Our hearts are:
One Heart Perfected.

Love is Loud

Our Hearts must have mouths,
for they seem to talk….
Their language is silence,

but their Love is Loud….
Like a sudden earthquake,
or a lightning thunderstorm….

Hunt of Love

Your piercing eyes,
tearing the veil of crowds,
hunt for my eyes —
like an angler hunting for a fish.

The angler lives not
 to relish the feast.
They both die in this
sweet Hunt of Love.

Love is all I deal with

If the doorway to your Heart
is through your eyes,
then gaze deeply,
lest you are afraid,
I would see through you.

THE SONG OF LOVE

My gaze will be sharp,
penetrating like ether.
It will reach your Heart.
My business is with the Heart,
Love is all I deal with.

Jewel of Love

At the Heart
of everything,
isn't it Love?

Atoms knitted
with the wool
of Love.

Planets orbiting
with the pull
of Love.

Lovers swimming
in the pool
of Love.

Observe everything
is so full
of Love.

In the Heart is
this Jewel
of Love.

The Freedom of Love

Glances fly
like birds,
they soar high
in the sky.

The freedom
in my wings
is nothing but
the Freedom of Love.

Love: The Heart's only Desire

Love is the Heart's
 only Desire….
Burning with
 this fire….
Our minds
 run into mire….
And suffer with
 world's ire….
Suffering and hankering
 desire after desire….
Not realizing heart's
 only desire….
Mind must turn
 inwards and enquire….
The only thing
 it must aspire….
Is Love: The Heart's
 only Desire….

Love is Worship

Some see it with wonder….
Some see it as a blunder….
For some, it roars like thunder….
To some, it leaves torn asunder….
Its touch is equal to plunder….
Love is Worship, no wonder….

THE SONG OF LOVE

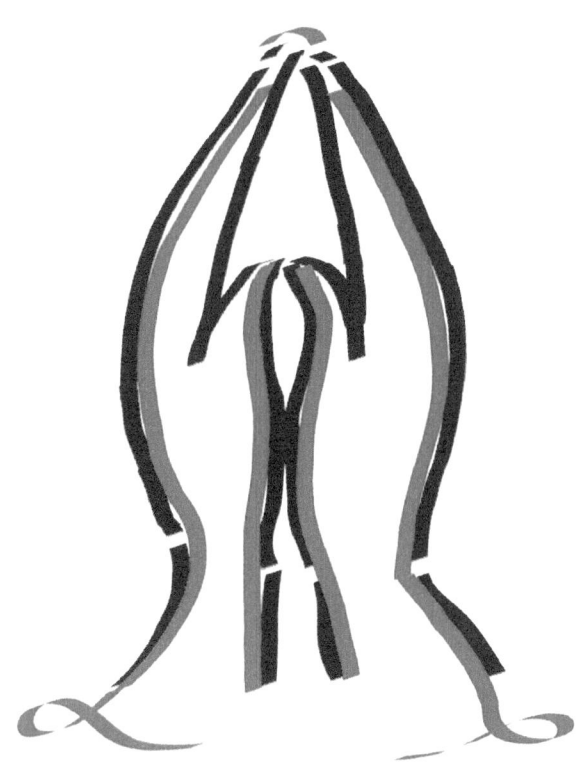

Harbinger of Love

Many a birth you took,
still knew not your true nature!
Many a time you were shook,
still rose not to your true stature!

Exerting and wading through life,
you die seeking nothing of worth.
Again you start running in strife,
coming back taking another birth.

Wake up now! Wake up anew!
Seek the Real within you.
Be the Peace! Be the Love!
You are the Harbinger of Love.

Love Is

Love Is —
It just Is….

You may
deny it,
and dare
try it….

You may
cover your eyes,
shut your mind
and act blind….

That which
encompasses all,
in comparison
everything is small….

Love Is —
It just Is….

In Love you are Born

Love is Alpha and Delta.
Love is Omega.
Love is Life and Death.
Love is Bodega.

In Love you are Born.
In Love you Die.
To Love you finally return,
with your last Peaceful Sigh.

Ambers of Love

Many a day
has gone by —
not seeing you
is as much yearning
as is seeing you.

In my Heart,
somewhere burn
these Ambers of Love.

The Gaze of Love

> My eyes have seen
> the melting in your eyes.
> Something melts inside,
> the moment I see you.

Are you sure
this is not the
melting of your Heart
with the Gaze of Love?

The Wine of Love

I speak of Love,
but I know not
what is this drunkenness!

> When I walk steady,
> I talk like a master,
> but the moment I fall,
> I realize my vulnerability.

In my walk,
and in my talk,
this stammering is the
Wine of Love.

Love is my Earning

O my Beloved,
my Soul's yearning....
You are the Heart,
its Eternal burning....

Your Love tears
the veil of Learning....
Worshipping is my Business,
Love is my Earning....

The Peace of Love

Oft times
you hear noises,
there are
way too many.

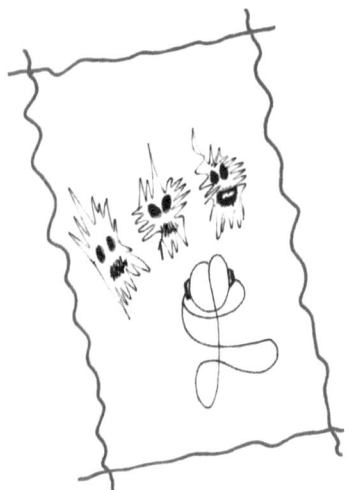

When the chattering
mind is gone,

a never ending
Peace is born.

The one that
always burns,
fragrant and warm,
is the incense of Love.

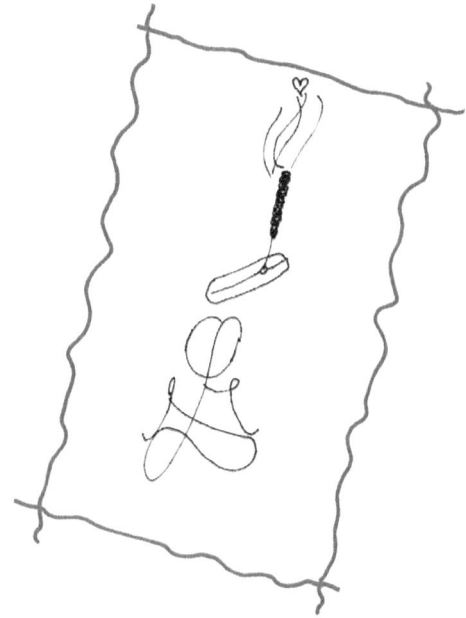

The one that
spreads like smoke,
yet soft and calm,
is the Peace of Love.

Offering of Love

My backpack
has many candies.
All are infused
with Divine Love.

Whomever I meet,
I like to offer.
Some take it,
others shun it.

It does not matter
who takes it.
All that matters is
my Offering of Love.

The Fruit of Love

What the Heart truly yearns,
and the longing that burns….
Stop the chase,
and Be Silent.

There is nowhere to go,
but in the Heart.
Your Beloved lives there,
there ends your search.

Many a birth you spent searching.
Nobody told you! — Go Inside. This is it.
In the orchard of your Heart,
now eat the Fruit of Love.

The True Worth of Love

And you thought
I understood Love!
Yes, but one percent,
that too I guess all wrong.

Love makes you worthy,
it ascends you to the sky,
it drops you from the cliff,
it keeps you busy.

One day you wake up
to realize who you are.
Love is all that you see
and realize the True Worth of Love.

Love Matures

Love is neither euphoria
nor it is any dysphoria.
Forgetting any modifications,
beyond any manifestations,
it is about an Awakened Being,
a calmed Breath, a pure Seeing.

THE SONG OF LOVE

Let me thus simply put it….
When the lamp of void is lit,
silence encompasses every bit,
armies of restlessness fully quit,
running, going, reaching stops,
the fruit of Love Matures and drops.

Fragrance of Love

Some call it as God,
some by other names.

Many are the names of
this Fragrance of Love.

The Essence of Love

Is Love pure white,
or is it pure black?

> Love must be white,
> a single dot ruins white.

> Love must be black,
> absorbs all the colors.

>> Love is none and all,
>> it is the color of colors.

That which shines forth,
is the Essence of Love.

The Touch of Love

Love's first touch is soft.
It slowly enters every marrow.

Now how to fly aloft?
The wretched poor sparrow!

She seems lost in Love.
This is the Touch of Love.

Love meets Love

Love's periphery must be round —
   When their Love is finally found —
Lovers revolve around and around —
   In each other's arms do they surround.

Earth is round, Sun is round —
   Earth revolves in its orbit around —
Like lovers revolve around and around —
   In each other's arms do they surround.

Life is round, Death is round —
   In cycles of existence are they found —
Like lovers revolve around and around —
   In each other's arms do they surround.

Fragments we are, in time we are bound —
   From day to night, time also hops around —

One leap and we cross the final round —
 This is where Love meets Love around.

The Desert of Love

Wandering you are
in this mirage.

The moment you see
a reflection,
you run after it
to quench your thirst.

Welcome to the
Desert of Love.

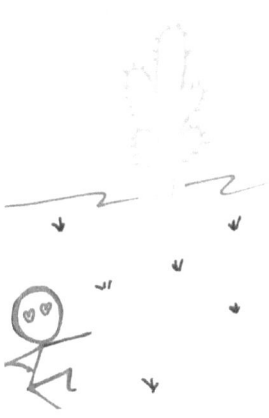

The God of Love

Love is an open space,
infinite and mysterious,
expanse beyond expanse,
self-evident and miraculous.

Breath-giving is this Love,
breath taking is this miracle,
self-existent, without below or above,
darkness of darkness, light at its pinnacle.

The one who lives in the Heart,
the one who loves in the Heart,
in the Lotus of that Heart,
abides the God of Love.

The Time of Love

Here nothing lives forever.
Everything time devours.

When time ceases,
that is the Time of Love.

The Illusions of Love

World is a mad house.
All the people of the world
are mad for something.

As if trying to catch hold
of the horns of a camel
in the snow of the Mount Everest.

Until the veil on the Heart is lifted,
mire in the Illusions of Love.

The Play of Love

How else do you think
galaxies are hanging in space?

Earth orbiting around the Sun!
Or stars disappearing as black holes!

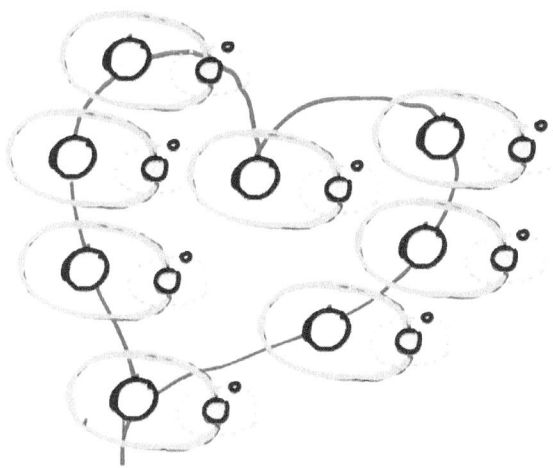

What for all this Play?
This is the Play of Love.

Lover of Love

I don't know
what Love is!

The more I talk,
the less I know!

Is there a
Knower of Love?

OR

Is there a
Lover of Love?

Waves of Love

Our lives are
like a child's markings
on a beach sand.

A strong surge of water,
and everything washes away.

How else could new markings
be made by new children?

Love is a flowing stream,
it cleanses everything in its way.

No markings are left behind
by the Waves of Love.
The ever flowing — Waves of Love.

Abode of Love

My Heart calls: I Love You,
twenty-four seven, it is true.
My meditations are full of your name.

> Why do you play such a game?
> Why do you play such a game?

You play with me Hide and Seek.
You are always hidden, and I seek.
I sit silent, my Heart does the job.

> With your Love, does it throb.
> With your Love, does it throb.

Loving you keeps my Heart busy.
Loving you keeps my Heart easy.
I wouldn't go below or above.

>This is my only — Abode of Love.
>This is my only — Abode of Love.

The Whole of Love

My words are drying.
Even if the ink be perpetual,
how must one express
the inexpressible and perennial!

How else to talk about infinity,
words can't catch hold of it!
How can a bucket capture eternity,
by whom billions of suns are lit!

Let me quench my own thirst,
and fill my little bucket of love.
Maybe by filling my little bucket,
I will fulfill the Whole of Love.

Eternity of Love of Eternity

Lord of the lords
Cord of the cords
You tie it all together
You untie it all to gather

When the sleep is over
The play is also over
Thy name is eternal
All else is ephemeral

I pray to thee
To liberate us into Eternity
Liberate us into thy
Eternity of Love of Eternity

In the Arms of Love

Instrument of Love,
is body's flute.
It starts to play,
when breath is en route.

Music of Love,
in silence it plays.
Rhythms of Love,
are in Love's praise.

Sing my Love sing,
thy songs of Love.
Many a day has passed,
now sing thy Love.

THE SONG OF LOVE

Nothing else is worthy,
but thy Love whirling.
Sing and dance thy Heart,
don't stop, keep swirling.

This is your appointed task,
the Task of Love.
This is how you die,
In the Arms of Love.

Love's Ode

Love is Heart's religion.
Mind's religion is reason.

Until reason is satisfied,
Mind does not subside.

Only when does mind surrender,
Peace comes in full splendor.

In the Heart's loving abode,
Peace sings Love's Ode….

The Imagination of Love

It takes two to Love —
A Lover and a Beloved.
And both are within us.
Then who makes love?
And to whom?
And what is the outcome?

A child or a figment?
A child must be a figment....
And so must be
the infinite worlds....
Figments of the
Imagination of Love....

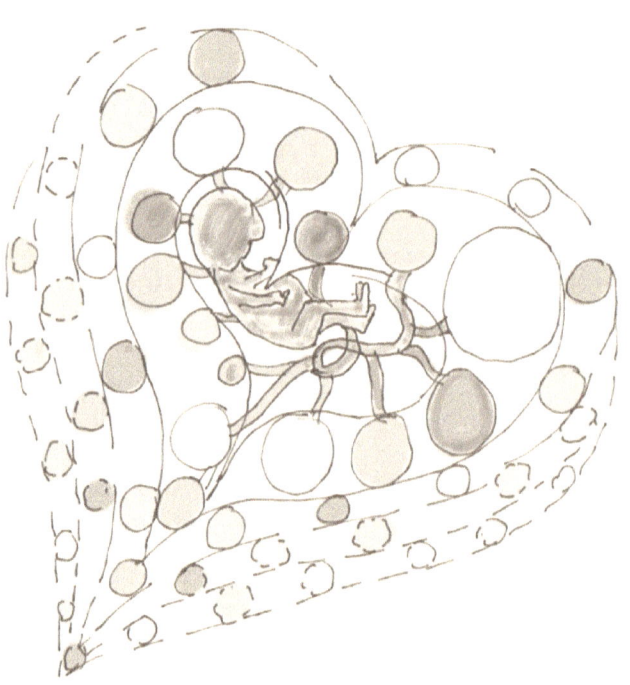

Nutrition of Love

Like food and water,
I eat and drink Love.
My nutrition is incomplete
without the breath of Love.

A fresh breath day and night
is all I need to survive.
If I am ill or dying, breathe
some Love, I may revive.

Examine yourself closely,
you may have similar needs.
Ego doesn't want you to accept,
then how to know where it bleeds!

You die thinking, what a wasted life,
when all you need is Love.
It's still time, eat & drink Love,
like I do, my Nutrition of Love.

Hearts of Love

Full I was when fast asleep....
Awakened grew emptiness deep....

Empty you make, in whom you peep....
In whose Hearts you gently bleep....

Their Hearts take a quantum leap....
Hearts of Love is what they reap....

THE SONG OF LOVE

Let there be Love

Every desire is a fog
on the mirror of the Heart.
Wipe clean the mirror,
Let there be Love.

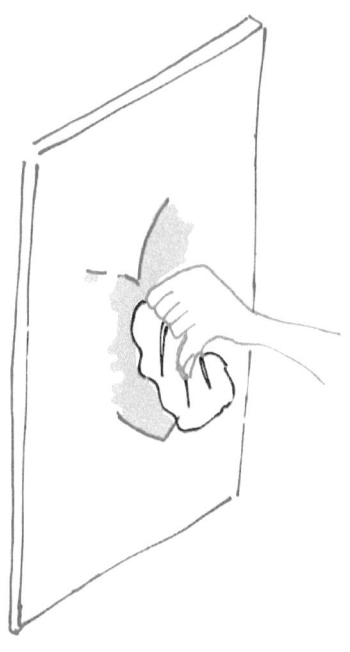

Emanations of Love

I decided to find the Beauty!
What is it that is so dear to me?
What in my beloved does attract?
Let me find out, let me dissect.

I thus mentally entered the body.
Perfect creation is but all shoddy.
Five senses are all full of worldly sins.
Stomach, kidneys are all garbage bins.

Beautiful long tresses and hairs of nose.
Like thorns coming out of a beautiful rose.
There are organs of pleasure and lusting.
Vessels and veins carry fluids disgusting.

Where to find Beauty? I entered the brain.
Full of spider webs of neurons, all in vain.
From all the nine doors, wastes come and go.
I then entered the Heart, its flesh pulsating to-and-fro.

What I find there is only blood gushing.
The blood in veins in and out flushing.
I went again but came back around.
Yet Beauty was nowhere to be found.

What were those eyes pulling me in?
Where resides that Beauty beyond skin?
I then entered the great Spiritual Heart.
Somewhere midst of the chest is this art.

It was most beautiful there.
Love was flowing like air.
Pulsating it was everywhere.
My unknown name was its affair.

Every breath came with my name.
Every breath left with my name.
This is where resides real Beauty.
Love's everlasting playful duty.

Now I found the whole body as Love.
From top to bottom it emanated Love.
Love was flowing in every tiny vein.
Love was flowing in Heart and brain.

Love was emanating from all the senses five.
Stomach, kidneys, organs were in Love's hive.
Every part of the body was now emanating Love.
Pulsating everything was with Emanations of Love.

Escapes of Love

Love is not —
what a poet writes about,
those are mere scribbles.

Love is that —
which after all the efforts,
manages to escape the pen.

Love shows itself —
only in the cave of one's Heart,
and escapes the pen of a bard.

In short —
these are the
Escapes of Love.

Love, let's Love

Days are passing by,
without the touch of Love.
Love is too precious.
Let's not waste time,
Love, let's Love.

The Flower of my Heart
feeds on Beloved's Love.
Without Love's fertilizer,
this Flower will wither.
Love, let's Love.

My Heart gets hungry
a little too soon.
It is a hoarder of Love.
Don't be a miser.
Love, let's Love.

The Name of Love

The name that
sounds and resounds
with every breath
in the cave of the Heart
is the Name of Love….

The Bird of Love

When the Heart regains
its pure primitive state….

Breath frees from its shackles
and natural ecstasy reigns….

The Bird of Love flies freely
in a Peaceful Blissful Heart….

Love is a Kite

Love is a Kite.
Its thread is in
unknown hands.

> It takes time to
> ascend into skies.

Slowly Love ascends
in the Sky of the Heart.

Once up there,
it flows freely.

Once the Kite
of Love flies freely,
there is Liberation.

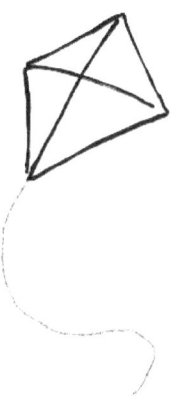

Love is Waiting

Keep not waiting
Go to your Beloved
Love flows everywhere
Wherever the Beloved is
Waste not this moment
Lest it goes into hiding
Go to your Beloved
Love is Waiting

What Love Wants

Love is patient.
It can wait forever.
It waited when
you had not arrived.
It waited when
you died many times,
without realizing Love.
It waited for lifetimes
for you to wake up.
Now you woke up
and realized Love,
Love will merge
you into itself.
This merging is
What Love Wants.
For this merging,
Love created you
in the first place.

Love is Heart's Journey

Love is Heart's Journey….

    from itself towards itself….

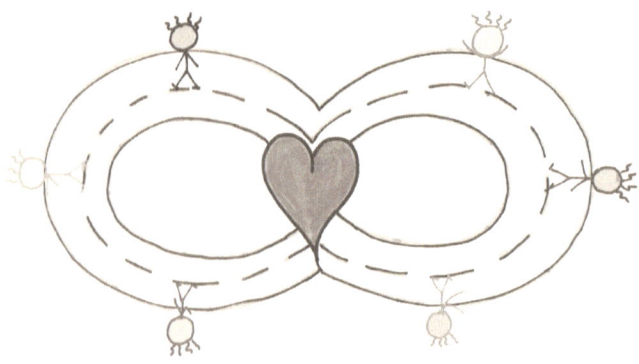

In between are stopovers….

    the traveler finally returns Home.

The Abode of Love

You do this tantra.
With a pure Heart,
continuously recite
this beautiful mantra —
<< Love, Love, Love >>
Eventually you shall attain
the Abode of Love.

The Elements of Love

When it comes,
it comes like a Tsunami,
entering every pore,
like Water does.

When it stays,
it erupts like a Volcano,
burning every corner,
like Fire does.

If it leaves,
it leaves like a Hurricane,
leaving turbulence behind,
like Air does.

Earth and Sky watch
the very play of the elements,
watching forever their wrath and
their settling into Peace.

These are nothing but
the Elements of Love.

The Mirror of Love

You said you polish,
but polishing iron
protects only from rust.

You need to first
make yourself into a glass,
transparent and fragile.
Only cleansing won't do,
but a complete transformation.
Once the transformation is done,
in the void of your being,
the hands of Love
will then coat you with
silver layers of Love.

Wait and behold!
You are the Mirror of Love,
reflecting utmost beauty.

Love reflects only Love

Once you are a Mirror of Love,
others will look into you
and say, "How beautiful!"
This they say
but for themselves.

Once they go away,
beauty disappears.
They realize not that
they just looked into
the Mirror of Love.

Whatever you place in front of it,
the Mirror of Love reflects only Love.

The Nightingale of Love

Love is Heart's Song,
sung in the Silence of Being.
Without this Silence,
there is no Song.

First be utterly Silent,
then will the mystery unfold.
The Nightingale of Love
will perch and sing.

THE SONG OF LOVE

How do I know?
I have seen the mystery unfold.

The Incense of Love

Has the search started yet,
or is the slumber too deep?
For the search to begin,
one must be shaken asleep.

When the fire starts burning the forest,
creatures run everywhere in chaos.
The Heart's fire does that to the mind,
and mind runs everywhere in chaos.

When the fire turns the mind to ashes,
then spreads the Incense of Love.
Before that you won't understand it,
how much ever you talk about Love.

There is Love

May thy breath
be thy guide,
for breath reaches
the inner corners.

May thy mind
be thy guide,
for mind causes
its own extinction.

When thy breath
and thy mind,
both give way,
There is Love.

Love Blooms

If you are still seeking,
 you haven't arrived yet.

If you want enlightenment,
 you haven't arrived yet.

Where Love blossoms,
 wants must disappear.

Love's soil only grows Love,
 desires are ego's thorns.

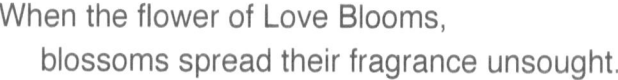

When the flower of Love Blooms,
 blossoms spread their fragrance unsought.

Eternal Love

When your mind is
    established permanently
        in the Silence of Being,
            then is the Eternal Love.

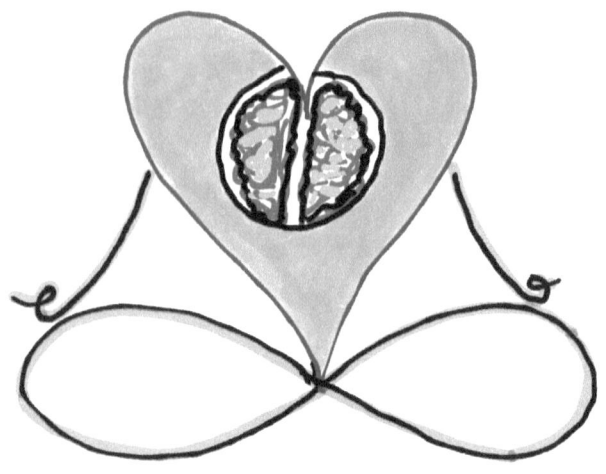

The dance and
the romance of
the Pure Consciousness
is the Eternal Love.

THE SONG OF LOVE

Love's Gifts

My Love for thee
is like a birdsong,
when it sings,
it rejoices in freedom.
When it stops,
it relaxes in silence.
Freedom and Silence
are Love's Gifts.

The Doors of Love

When I knocked
the Doors of Love —
Came the reply: "Who?"
I said, "I."
The doors remained shut.

I knocked again —
Came the reply: "Who?"
I said, "YOU."
The doors remained shut.

I knocked again —
Came the reply: "Who?"
I said, "WE."
The doors remained shut.

I knocked again —
Came the reply: "Who?"
I remained utterly silent,
and lo! the doors ope wide….

The Silence of the Being
is the key to the Doors of Love.

Love's Demands

Love's Demands are simple,
it just doesn't want you.
The "You" in you must vanish,
only then Love comes.
The doors of << I AM >> must open
for Love to enter the Heart.

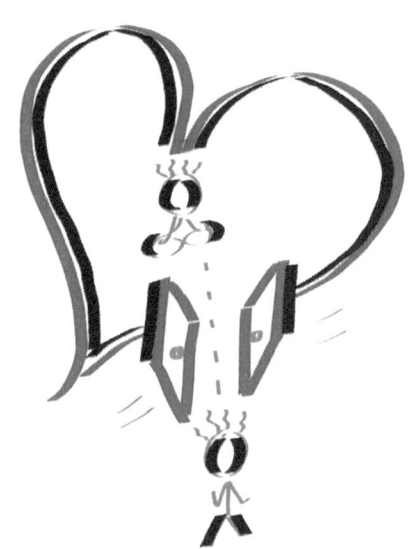

Love of the Finite

Love of the finite,
must be finite.
Love of the infinite,
must be infinite.

The transition from
the finite to the infinite
requires transformation,
and Love of the Finite.

The Fabric of Love

The very Fabric
   of the Universe,
is a special
   Fabric of Love.
Woven with Love,
   interwoven threads
exhibit immense beauty.

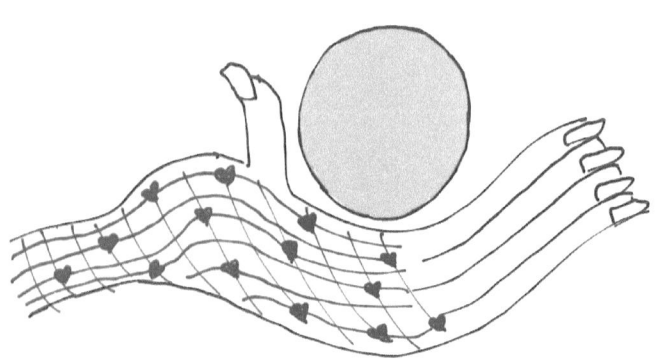

These interwoven threads
are our relationships.
Entanglements are
caused by desires.
Freedom from them
is our ability to Love.

Love I Enshrine

I wait for your glimpse,
and you for mine.
My Heart is in yours,
and yours is in mine.
Still this longing to see you
sustains, how asinine!
I could never understand,
this Love I Enshrine.

I Became Love

Your eyes spoke
with mine eyes.
They were saying
silently but loudly,
I Love You….
I Love You….

In your eyes,
I saw your Heart.

In your Heart,
I saw your Love.
In your Love,
I saw the Eternal.
In the Eternal,
I Became Love.

May I return to Love

May the journey of
many a birth cease.
In your lap,
let me die in Peace.

My quest is over,
I am in natural ease.
In your arms,
let me die in Peace.

May I return to Love,
the abode of final release.
In your embrace,
let me die in Peace.

This Rose of Love

That I call a Rose,
is beautiful at Heart.
Soft are its petals,
yet its thorns are sharp.

> That I call Love,
> is simplicity at Heart.
> Soft is its touch,
> yet its pangs are sharp.

To thee thus I offer
this Rose of Love,
so you know not
only the soft touch
that makes you fly,
but also the pangs
that make you cry.

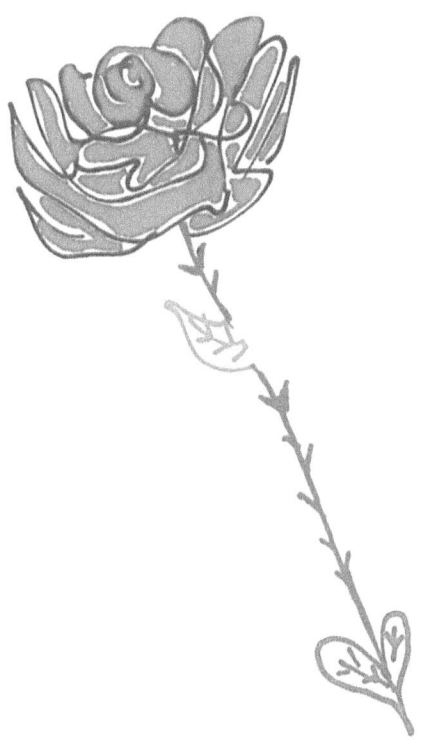

To thee I offer my Heart:
This Rose of Love,
so its sufferings thrash open
thy inner door of beauty,
and its soft touch
eases you into its Peace.
For thee is this Rose of Love.

Love Forever

Where boundaries disappear,
where neither I
nor You exist.

></br>
> Where no thoughts arise,
> in that silent submission,
> no interpretations persist.

></br>
></br>
> In that state
> of silent awareness,
> may we Love Forever.

Love is Full Circle

I was born
in your image.

In you,
I worshipped myself.

In me,
You worshipped yourself.

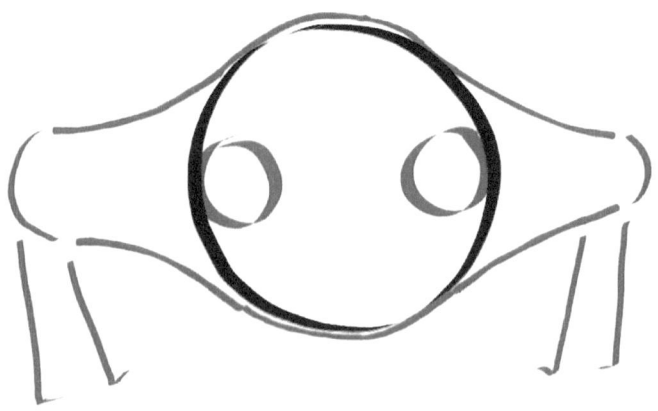

From Love begins
this journey,
to Love it returns.
Love is Full Circle.

Love is Nigh

In the end,
we all die.
One thing that
we barely try,
Is Love….

For it seems a lie,
all our desires
burn us dry,
leading us farther,
even if Love is Nigh.
In between,
we laugh and cry.

In the end,
we all die.
One thing that
we barely try,
Is Love….

Love's Command

On the crossroads,
we meet again.
As strangers meet
in a bus or a train.

> After dying for ages,
> lo! we are born again.
> Subconsciously knowing
> of our Love and pain.

The very first sight
binds them again.
The Love flowing
in their eyes-twain.

> Do we know? Questions
> their heads contain.
> Their Hearts know it all,
> heads contend and drain.

Their Hearts communicate
through some intuitive brain.
Their Hearts are tied as if
by an invisible immortal chain.

> They feel subtle energies
> of some invisible domain.
> Their Love travels freely
> across territories and terrain.

How could silent glances
of strangers sustain,
without knowing previously
the memories they contain?

> How is it all possible
> without Love's ordain?
> All this mystery is possible,
> as this is the Heart's domain.

On the crossroads,
when we meet again,
Love's Command is all
we abide by and sustain.

Love's Rosary

Love's path,
to the intersection
it leads.

Where one Heart,
with its counterpart
it meets.

In some divine silence,
one talks to the other
and greets.

Their Love is their Rosary,
their Hearts,
its beads.

Their mutual devotion,
towards emancipation
it leads.

Love is the Ultimate Music

The flute says
to the flutist….

My body fills
with thy Love

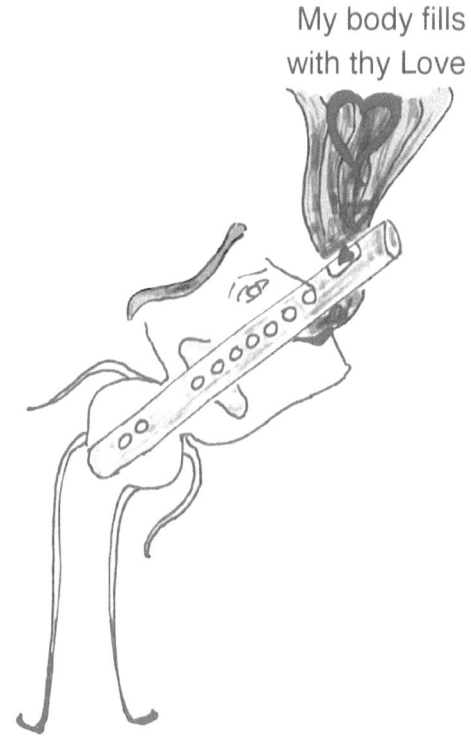

and dances at
thy fingertips.

This body has
no meaning
unless it is filled
with thy Love.

Thy Love is
the Ultimate Music,
playing the notes
of thy divinity.

One God of Love

The center of the Universe,
the center of the Earth,
and the center of my Being
are all inside Me.

That which you call "The Heart,"
is the core of all.
<< I AM >> the center from which
all this originates.

The God of Love
resides inside my Heart.
All our hearts
are God's Heart.

There is One Heart
in all the hearts.
In all the diversity,
there is One God of Love.

The Tug of Love

Betwixt these
    pairs of eyes
        is the Tug of Love.

When one's pull is strong,
    the other is drawn,
        and vice versa.

This Tug of Love
is poetry in action.
It is the pull of God.

Reflection of Love

Mind is a kaleidoscope,
forming illusive patterns
on the mirror of the Heart.

Wipe clean the mirror and
the calm Reflection of Love
will shine on its surface.

Love's Path

Love's Path
is the path

>on which
>only one walks

>and that too
>without footsteps….

The Dark Night of Love

When Heart's flower blossoms fully,
    Love's petals spread wide.

In this blossoming
    is hidden Love's pain
        that the Heart endures.

When the bird of the Heart matures,
    Love spreads its wings wide.

In this expanse
    is the Dark Night of Love,
        before the Heart matures.

Love is the Sun

In the Heart's Cave
resides darkness.

Only Love can Light
its deepest recesses.

Love is the Lamp
of the Heart's Hidden Cave.

Love is the Sun
of the Heart's Solar System.

Love is all we have

A sudden vibration
in Nothingness,
spreads into an
Infinite Expansion….

A sudden vibration
in the Heart,
spreads into an
All-Encompassing Love….

Worlds within worlds,
dance to its tunes.
In short: Love is
all we have….

To Love and to get Lost

A thousand times better
is to Love and to get Lost,
than rationally wading your way
through Life's endless maze.

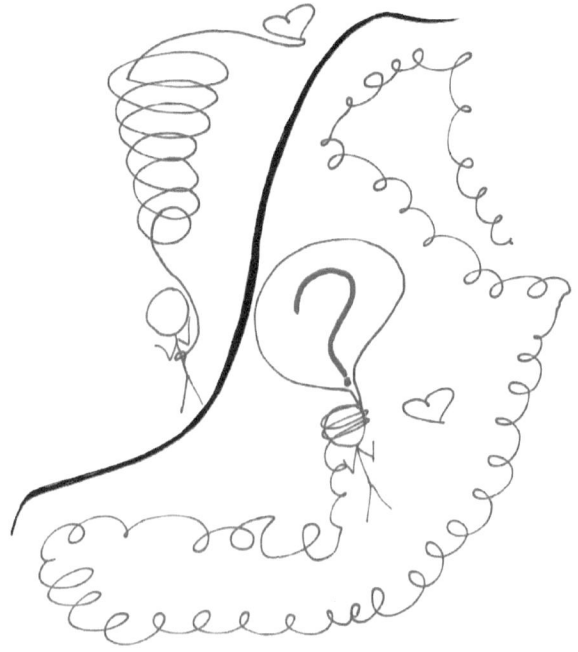

Closer you may be to the end
when Love leaves you astray,
while your rational meanderings
may lead you farther away.

Love is the Primal Force

In thy Love
I dissolve….
like sugar
in water….

Love is the
Primal Force,
the pot and
the potter.

No separation
do I see,
twixt the son
and the father.

The unknowable reality,
ever present,
the creatrix of
matter-antimatter.

Love is in Simple Things

Love is in Simple Things.
When somewhere a bird sings,
or a bud blossoms and springs,
look closely Love's hidden strings.

When a little kid walks,
in her divinity she talks.
When in anger a person yells,
Love's burning energy one smells.

When you laugh, Love Is….
When you suffer, Love Is….
When you do whatever you do….
Love is silently carrying you….

In the Honor of Love

Millions of stars....
  Millions of galaxies....
All serve thy honor....
  All sing thy glories....

In whose dreams....
  do they arise as stories....
Then merge back....
  and become mere reveries....

In this dream of yours....
  I woke up from fantasies....
To sing in thy honor....
  To sing thy glories....

What else is the way
  to the beyond-above?
Isn't it to sing ceaselessly
  In the Honor of Love?

The Infinity of Love

Many a poem
Many a song
Many a bell
Many a gong….

Sing thy glory
All fall short
For thy expanse
Can never be reached
With words or sounds….

The Lord of
The Unstuck Sound
Can never be tied
In limits or bounds….

This Infinite Expanse
Is the Infinity of Love….

Love is the greatest Phoenix

I prayed Love
to visit me
and fill this
frail empty vessel.

> Love visited me
> and bared open
> all that was
> hidden underneath.

My chest was
torn apart
and the deluge
filled my Heart.

> At Love's first kiss,
> I ran in excitement.
> Slowly pain took over
> and then wretchedness.

I am not sure
if asking for Love
was too naive
or too wishful.

> Still collecting I am,
> the torn shreds
> that Love left me in
> after its fateful visit.

Be careful what
you really ask for.
Divine Love is the
greatest Phoenix.

> It will lure you,
> burn you to ashes,
> and if you are still worthy,
> it may erect you.

From ashes
to resurrection,
Love's journey runs through
nailing you to the Cross.

THE SONG OF LOVE

This weird thing called Love

All this is a dream,
and so are these poems.

Everything is made up of
the same material of illusion.

Nothing stays forever,
everything time devours.

But there is this
weird thing called Love!

How everything comes out of it?
I don't understand that.

THE SONG OF LOVE

I must have Loved

The Universe
is a place
for Lovers….

How do I know?

I must have Loved
and Found.

The Love's Show

Our lives are –
the Love's Show...
For Love –
they flow...
In Love –
they grow...
To Love –
they go...

ABOUT THE AUTHOR

You, the Lover,
would be developing relations
with Me, the Lover,
through my Heart's creations.

Call me not a poet nor compare.
Eternal Love is all I have to share.
We can talk about Me some other time.
For now, let's talk about Love sublime.

www.ingramcontent.com/pod-product-compliance
Lightning Source LLC
Chambersburg PA
CBHW021106080526
44587CB00010B/402